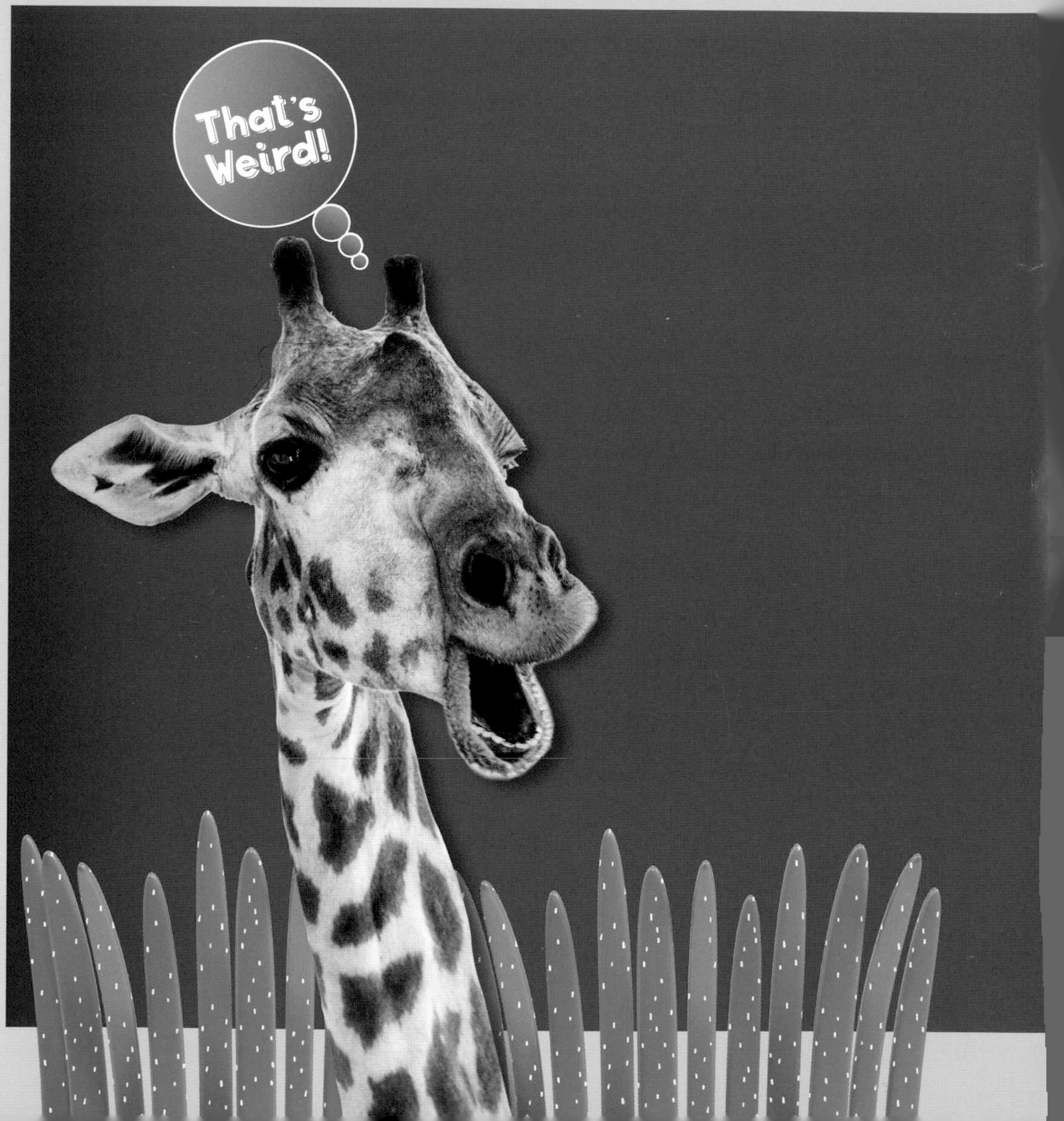
That's Weird!

NATIONAL
GEOGRAPHIC
KiDS

weird but true! 3

350 OUTRAGEOUS FACTS

NATIONAL GEOGRAPHIC
WASHINGTON, D.C.

Octopuses
have
three
hearts.

THE UNIVERSE IS ABOUT 13.7 BILLION YEARS OLD.

KANGAROOS CAN JUMP MORE THAN 30 FEET (9 m) IN ONE HOP. THAT'S THE LENGTH OF 12 SKATEBOARDS!

STUDIES SHOW THAT WHEN EVENLY MATCHED TEAMS COMPETE, THE TEAM WEARING RED HAS A BETTER CHANCE OF WINNING.

One of the shortest wars ever lasted

FAN FACT! SUBMITTED BY MITCHELL S., 9

There was a hotel made of garbage in Rome, Italy.

The Earth spins so fast that someone standing at the

Equator is traveling at about 1,000 miles an hour.

(1,600 km/h)

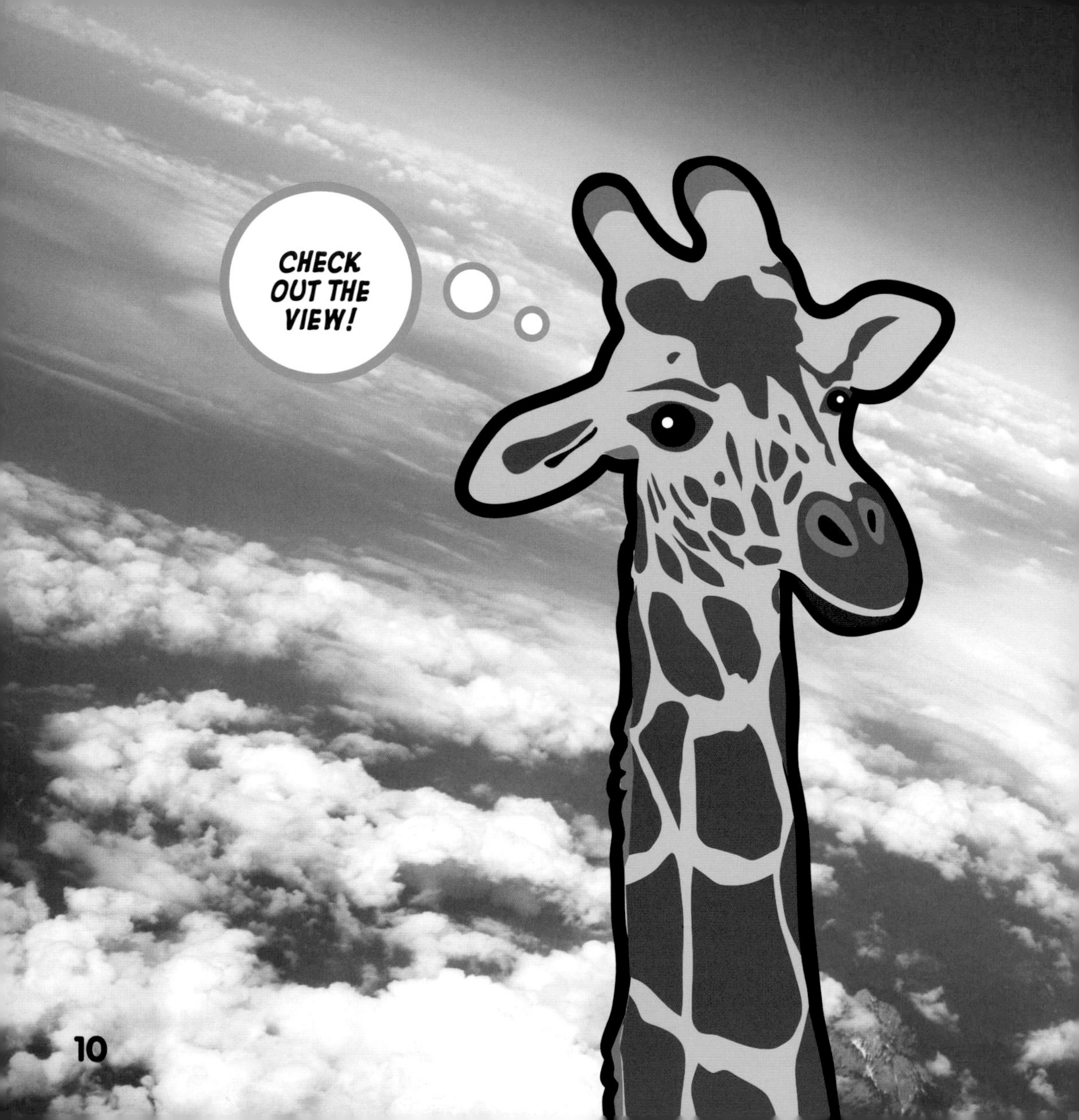
CHECK OUT THE VIEW!

It would take a **stack** of more than **100,000 giraffes** to reach the outermost layer of the Earth's atmosphere.

The Earth weighs about 6,600,000,000,000,000,000,000,000 metric tons.

(1 metric ton=2,204.6 pounds)

Legend says that Aztec ruler **Moctezuma** drank 50 cups of hot chocolate a day.

YOU LOSE UP TO 100 HAIRS A DAY.

ELEPHANTS CAN RUN FASTER THAN HUMANS.

A warm frog makes faster croaking noises **than a cold frog.**

THE FIRST AIRPLANE JOURNEY ACROSS THE UNITED STATES TOOK 49 DAYS.

SEEING THE COLOR RED CAN MAKE YOUR HEART BEAT FASTER.

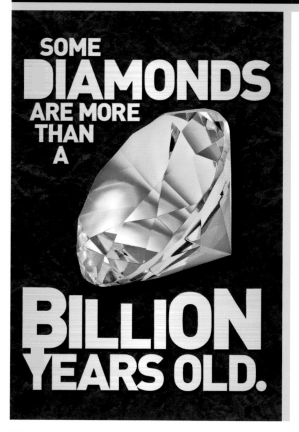

SOME **DIAMONDS** ARE MORE THAN A **BILLION** YEARS OLD.

IT'S **POSSIBLE** TO PRODUCE ELECTRICITY FROM **ELEPHANT DUNG.**

IF HUMANS CAME IN AS MANY SIZES AS DOGS, WE'D RANGE FROM **THREE** TO **EIGHTEEN** FEET TALL.

(91.4 cm to 5.5 m)

Some **astronauts** living on the Mir space station ate **Jell-O** every Sunday to help keep track of the days.

AN AVERAGE MAJOR LEAGUE **BASEBALL** IS USED FOR ONLY SIX PITCHES.

YOUR FEET HAVE 500,000 SWEAT GLANDS.

SAUCER-SHAPED LENTICULAR CLOUDS HAVE BEEN MISTAKEN FOR UFOS.

ALL THE
MINED GOLD
IN THE WORLD
CAN FILL TWO
OLYMPIC-SIZE
SWIMMING POOLS.

A **man** once ate **49** glazed **doughnuts** in **8 minutes.**

More than a thousand Earths could fit inside Jupiter.

IF YOU TRAVELED AS FAST AS A CAR ON THE HIGHWAY, IT WOULD TAKE NEARLY THREE DAYS AND NIGHTS TO REACH THE EARTH'S CORE.

DAYS WERE ONLY 18 HOURS LONG A BILLION YEARS AGO.

THERE ARE **HUNDRED-FOOT-TALL** (30 m) **SAND DUNES IN ALASKA.**

A queen bee can lay **2,000** eggs a day in the spring.

SCORPIONS GLOW UNDER BLACK LIGHT.

A woman's **heart** usually beats faster than a man's **heart.**

It's impossible to see a full rainbow in the sky at noon.

Some **FROGS** survive the winter by freezing almost solid.

Four-thousand-year-old popcorn

was found in a cave in New Mexico, U.S.A.

A lizard sticks its tongue out to smell.

In Italy, you can buy

from a
vending machine.

SATURN'S RINGS ARE MADE OF ICE AND ROCKS.

A gold-plated bicycle sold for £80,000 (\$125,344) in the U.K.

Sperm whales have the heaviest BRAINS on the planet.

A cat has about 20 muscles in each ear.

Certain sharks walk on their fins **underwater.**

Some moths drink the tears of elephants.

In the summer, the amount of water pouring over **Niagara Falls** (on the U.S.-Canada border) each second could fill 13,000 bathtubs.

Your brain is about three-quarters water.

Frog bones grow new rings as they age, just like trees.

Dirty snow melts faster than **clean snow.**

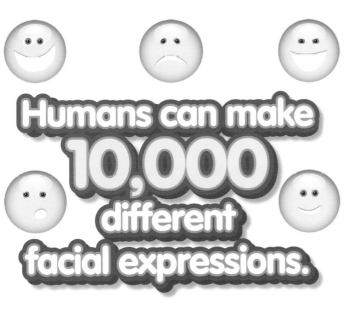

Humans can make **10,000** different facial expressions.

THE OLDEST **ROCKS** IN THE **GRAND CANYON** ARE ALMOST **TWO BILLION** YEARS OLD.

Cheetah ancestors roamed North America about four million years ago.

Every zebra's stripe pattern is different.

THE CORPSE FLOWER GROWS UP TO 12 FEET TALL (3.7 m) AND SMELLS LIKE ROTTING MEAT.

WHAT STINKS?

One of the world's **fastest snakes**—the **black mamba**—slithers up to **7** miles (11 km) an hour.

A MALE
AFRICAN CICADA CAN MAKE A SOUND AS LOUD AS A POWER MOWER.

A RIPE CRANBERRY WILL BOUNCE.

A company once sold a **cupcake-shaped** designer handbag— with strawberry- and-chocolate- colored crystals— **for $4,295.**

There is a **40**-FOOT (12-m)- tall steel statue of a **PRAYING MANTIS** that SHOOTS FLAMES from its ANTENNAE in downtown Las Vegas, Nevada, U.S.A.

You can get your **SELFIE** turned into **LATTE ART.**

NASA is designing a new fabric for astronauts that looks like the **CHAIN MAIL MEDIEVAL KNIGHTS WORE.**

A man spent **93 DAYS PADDLEBOARDING 4,000 MILES** from Africa to the Caribbean. (6,500 km)

A museum in Alaska, U.S.A., features an **OUTHOUSE** made of **ICE.**

A Japanese cat owner **MAKES HATS** for her pets **USING THEIR OWN FUR.**

Reading the word **"SUN"** can cause your **PUPILS TO GET SMALLER.**

BAMBOO SHARKS shrug their shoulders to help them **SWALLOW FOOD.**

44

Some **CLOUDS** are filled with **LOLLIPOP-SHAPED ICE CRYSTALS.**

An asparagus spear can grow **10 inches** (25 cm) in **24 hours.**

You can buy a **TENNIS-BALL-SIZE STRAWBERRY** in Japan for **$4,000.**

That's Weird!

AN ELEVATOR IN GERMANY can travel up and down, side to side, and diagonally.

IT IS ILLEGAL to have a **PET RAT** in Alberta, Canada.

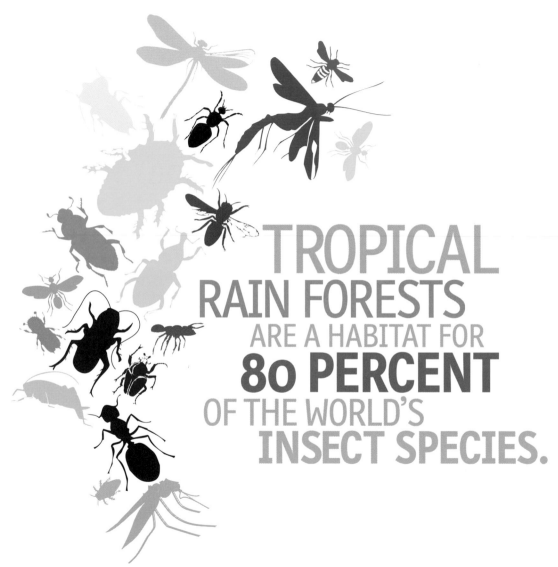

TROPICAL
RAIN FORESTS
ARE A HABITAT FOR
80 PERCENT
OF THE WORLD'S
INSECT SPECIES.

Mummies of ancient **Egyptian royalty** were wrapped in thousands of feet (meters) of bandages.

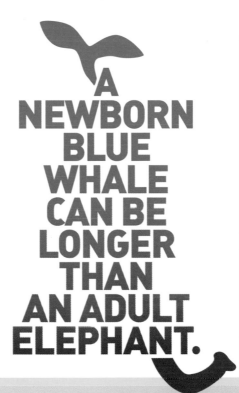

A NEWBORN BLUE WHALE CAN BE LONGER THAN AN ADULT ELEPHANT.

A camel's eye has **3** eyelids.

EVERY CONTINENT HAS A CITY CALLED ROME
(EXCEPT ANTARCTICA).

Newborn dolphins

sleep for only a few seconds at a time.

Earth's temperature rises slightly during a full moon.

MOUNT EVEREST IS ABOUT 27 TIMES TALLER THAN THE EIFFEL TOWER.

Yawns are contagious for **chimpanzees,** just as they are for **humans.**

Every (6.5 sq cm) **square inch of your skin** hosts about **6 million bacteria.**

BUTTERFLIES MUST WARM THEIR WINGS IN THE SUN BEFORE FLYING.

Guinea pigs can walk as soon as they are born.

FAN FACT! SUBMITTED BY ALEC S., 11

Your stomach would digest itself without mucus.

The world's longest known **crystal** is **37.4** feet long. (11.4 m) That's 8 times taller than an average 10-year-old.

An eagle's nest can s t r e t c h wider than your sofa.

HUMANS have lived on Earth for about **200,000** years; **DINOSAURS** walked the planet for roughly *160 million* years.

MORE THAN

99 PERCENT

OF THE SPECIES THAT
HAVE EVER EXISTED ARE NOW

EXTI

NCT.

Olive **oil** and **garlic** are **real** ice-cream flavors.

FAN FACT! SUBMITTED BY CARSON B., 11

Some pet spas serve catnip tea to feline guests.

Catnip Blend

Spit can *freeze in midair* at the North Pole.

LAIKA THE DOG WAS THE FIRST "ASTRONAUT" TO TRAVEL INTO SPACE.

THERE ARE
ABOUT
3,000
LIGHTNING
FLASHES
ON
EARTH
EVERY MINUTE.

SKUNKS HAVE STRIPED SKIN UNDER THEIR FUR.

Blondes have more hairs on their heads than brunettes.

THE BIGGEST KNOWN INTACT DINOSAUR SKULL

THE FIRST SPACE TOURIST PAID $20 MILLION FOR A TEN-DAY TRIP TO THE INTERNATIONAL SPACE STATION.

BOUQUETS
IN AUSTRIA HAVE AN ODD NUMBER OF **FLOWERS;** EVEN NUMBERS ARE CONSIDERED **BAD LUCK.**

IS L O N G E R THAN A **RACEHORSE'S BODY.**

The **bombardier beetle** can shoot hot **poison** from its rear end **500** times a second.

More men are color-blind than women.

Some sea stars break off their own arms when frightened.

YIKES!

The largest known ant supercolony stretches nearly 4,000 miles (6,440 km) through Portugal, Spain, France, and Italy.

The Hawaiian alphabet has only **13** letters.

YOU CAN BUY FAKE EYEBROWS AND EYELASHES MADE OUT OF REAL HAIR.

THE HARDER YOU CONCENTRATE,

THE LESS YOU BLINK.

Crocodiles sometimes walk on the backs of hippos.

A river in Canada once turned **red.**

SHALOM HEI BAREV KUMUSTA SALAAM KIA ORA
APA KHABAR NI HAO HALLO ZDRAVO
BONJOUR GOEDENDAG HUJAMBO HEI SA'LAM
YIA SOU TIENA YISTILIGN MINGALA BA
MBOTE **Nearly** BOM DIA SOUR SDEY
AHOJ! BOK XIN CHÀO
AHLAN WA SAHLAN **7,000** JÓ NAPOT
AKWAABA DIA DHUIT
MONI **languages** MALO
ANNYONG HASEYO SALEM
LABAS HOLA **are spoken** TERVIST
SABBAI DII SAIN BAINA UU
MERHABA **worldwide.** OI
VITAYU HALLÓ JAMA NGAA CZEŚĆ WHAH GWAAN
PRIVYET JAMBO KONNICHI WA HEJ
SAWATDEE NAMASTE BUNĂZIUA E KARO GRÜTSIE
CIAO MHOROI MBA'ÉICHAPA ASSALAMO ALAIKUM

ONE OF THE **WORLD'S LARGEST BUILDINGS** SITS ON A FAULT LINE IN TAIWAN; ITS WEIGHT MAY HAVE TRIGGERED SEVERAL EARTH-QUAKES.

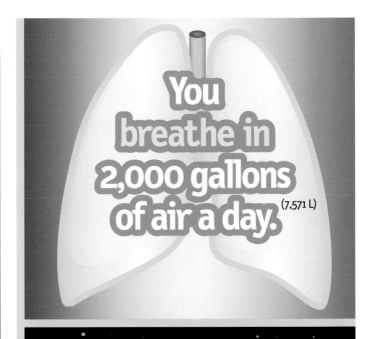

You breathe in 2,000 gallons of air a day. (7,571 L)

The world's largest menorah is taller than a three-story building.

MALE WOODCHUCKS ARE CALLED HE-CHUCKS;

FEMALES ARE CALLED SHE-CHUCKS.

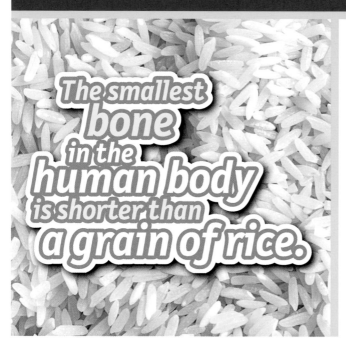

The smallest **bone** in the **human body** is shorter than **a grain of rice.**

CAMELS CHEW IN A FIGURE-EIGHT MOTION.

The oldest chocolate ever found was inside a 2,600-year-old pot in Belize.

STUDIES SHOW THAT PAINTING YOUR ROOM BLUE COULD MAKE YOU MORE CREATIVE.

A SHARK CAN LIVE FOR SIX WEEKS WITHOUT EATING.

THE WORLD'S POPULATION GROWS BY ABOUT A BILLION PEOPLE EVERY 12 YEARS.

Small icebergs are called growlers and bergy bits.

There was once a lake the size of England in the Sahara.

BLING!
BLING!

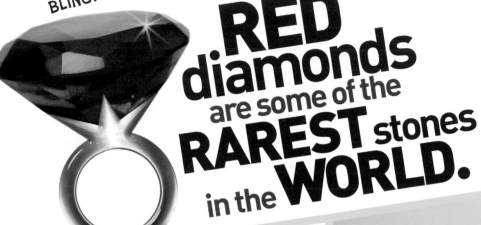

RED diamonds are some of the **RAREST** stones in the **WORLD.**

WARTHOGS DON'T HAVE WARTS.

SALT HAS BEEN USED AS MONEY.

THE SUN IS **400** TIMES LARGER THAN THE **MOON.**

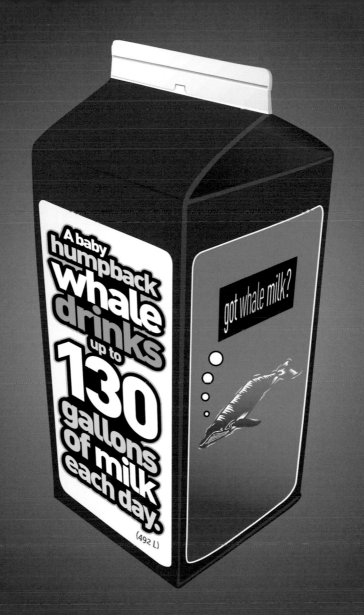

A baby humpback whale drinks up to 130 gallons of milk each day.

(492 L)

got whale milk?

Mantis shrimp can see colors better than humans can.

▲ **FAN FACT!** SUBMITTED BY RILEY C., 10

Australian Aboriginals,
the world's oldest
living culture,
have existed for at least
50,000 years.

astro h₂0

Astronauts drink recycled urine.

A METEORITE ONCE HIT A MAILBOX IN GEORGIA, U.S.A.

Parrots talk without vocal cords.

HAIR GROWS ALMOST EVERYWHERE ON YOUR **SKIN** EXCEPT YOUR LIPS, THE PALMS OF YOUR HANDS, AND THE SOLES OF YOUR FEET.

Months that begin on **SUNDAYS** always have a Friday the 13th.

Rats can't **burp.**

TEST FLIGHTS OF THE

FIRST SPACE SHUTTLE

TOOK OFF FROM THE

BACK OF A

FLYING 747.

Scientists think substances found in **SEAWEED** could be used to **EXTEND THE LIFE OF CELL PHONE BATTERIES.**

A 400-YEAR-OLD SILK DRESS was recently **RECOVERED FROM A SHIPWRECK** in the North Sea.

The force of a **COCONUT CRAB'S PINCH** is stronger than **CRUSHING YOUR TOE** under a **REFRIGERATOR.**

A coffee-pot-shaped water tower in California, U.S.A., could hold the equivalent of **1.28 MILLION CUPS OF COFFEE.**

WHEN SEAHORSES ARE ANGRY, THEY "GROWL."

A model of the **GREEK PARTHENON** on display in Germany is made of **STEEL, PLASTIC, AND 100,000 BANNED BOOKS.**

The **LIGHTS ON A BRIDGE** in Montreal, Canada, **CHANGE COLOR** at night **based on the day's weather, traffic, and news.**

There is a **WORLD** championship for best **LATTE ART.**

A GLASS-BOTTOM INFINITY POOL HANGS OFF A BUILDING **500 FEET** (152 m) **ABOVE A STREET** IN HOUSTON, TEXAS, U.S.A.

THE WORLD'S LONGEST MARBLE RUN was **6,293 FEET** (1,918 m) and **STRETCHED ACROSS A SMALL TOWN IN SWITZERLAND.**

A nearly **2,000-year-old loaf of bread** was found during excavations of **Italy's Mount Vesuvius.**

That's Weird!

An **ELEPHANT SEAL** can recognize a rival **by the TEMPO** of its **CALL.**

Dolphins may be smarter

than chimpanzees.

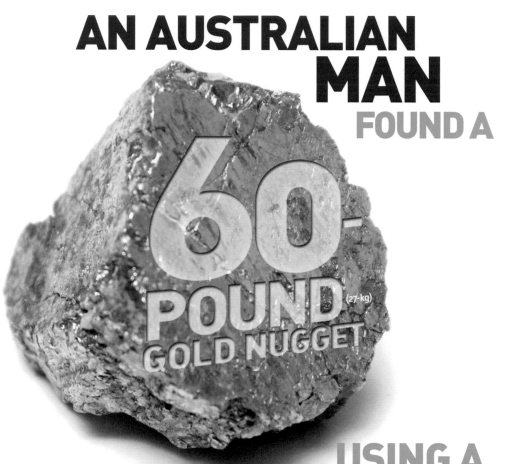

AN AUSTRALIAN MAN FOUND A 60-POUND (27-kg) GOLD NUGGET USING A METAL DETECTOR.

Chromophobia is the extreme fear of colors.

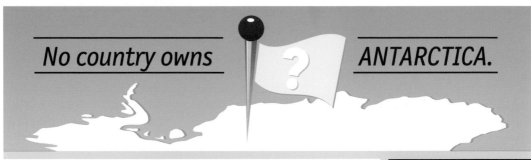

No country owns ANTARCTICA.

AT A RESTAURANT IN MICHIGAN, U.S.A., YOU CAN ORDER A SUPERSIZE HAMBURGER THAT WEIGHS AS MUCH AS A GROWN MAN.

Most spiders have 8 eyes.

90

SOME PEOPLE CAN HEAR THEIR EYEBALLS MOVING.

Most swans in England belong to the Queen.

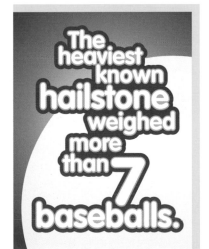

The heaviest known hailstone weighed more than 7 baseballs.

Some **CLOUDS** are more than **10 miles** (16 km) **TALL.**

A beaver's home is called a lodge.

SATURN HAS MORE THAN **60** MOONS.

It takes **three liters** of freshwater to make **one liter** of bottled water.

COULD YOU SPEAK UP?

A praying mantis has only one ear.

The north pole of **Uranus** gets no **sunlight** for about **42 years** at a time.

ALL OF THE PEOPLE ON EARTH

COULD CROWD INTO HALF
THE COUNTRY OF BELGIUM.

THE WORLD'S BIGGEST ROCK,

ULURU

IN AUSTRALIA,
IS TALLER THAN A
114-STORY BUILDING.

A geep is part goat, part sheep.

There are more pets in **Japan** than children.

SMELLING GOOD SCENTS, SUCH AS ROSES, WHEN YOU SLEEP MAY GIVE YOU HAPPY DREAMS.

A goldfish will turn gray if kept in the dark for a long time.

ANCIENT GREEKS USED **hula hoops.**

About 95 percent of the stuff in the universe is invisible.

HORSES CAN TRAVEL UP TO (160 km) 100 MILES IN A DAY.

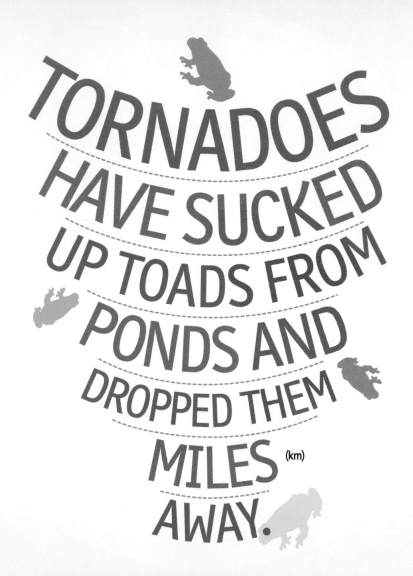

TORNADOES HAVE SUCKED UP TOADS FROM PONDS AND DROPPED THEM MILES (km) AWAY.

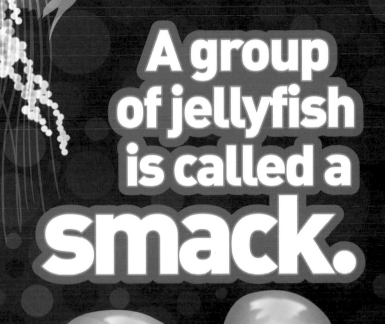

A group of jellyfish is called a **smack.**

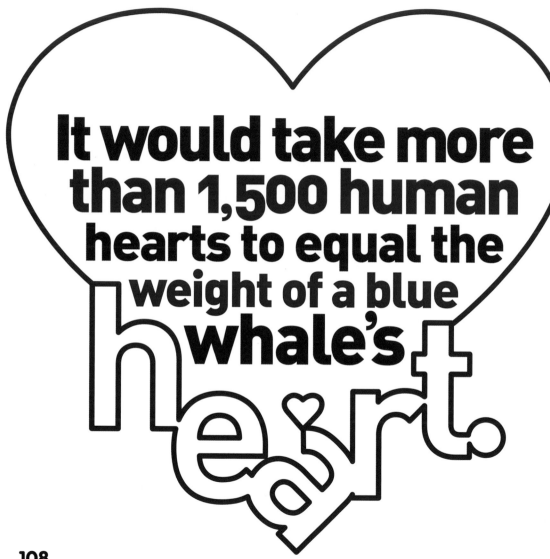

It would take more than 1,500 human hearts to equal the weight of a blue whale's heart.

SOME GEESE CAN SOAR TO 32,000 FEET— (9,750 m)
HIGH ENOUGH TO SEE A 747 PASSENGER JET FLY BY.

The surface of the moon is smaller than Asia.

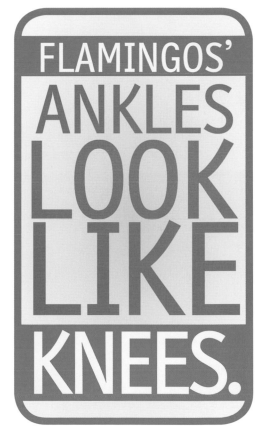

FLAMINGOS' ANKLES LOOK LIKE KNEES.

OUR UNIVERSE HAS NO CENTER.

The oldest **koi fish** lived to be

230

years old.

A **ROCK PYTHON** CAN LIVE FOR A YEAR WITHOUT A MEAL.

THERE ARE VOLCANOES INSIDE SOME GLACIERS.

It's impossible for turtles to stick out their tongues.

YOU CAN BUY SOAP THAT SMELLS LIKE BACON FRYING.

A hamster's teeth never stop growing.

THE OLDEST KNOWN PINE TREE IS MORE THAN 5,000 YEARS OLD.

FAN FACT! SUBMITTED BY ISABEL M., 8

Some of the most expensive **rocks on Earth** come from the **moon.**

A GIRAFFE HAS THE SAME NUMBER OF NECK BONES THAT YOU DO: SEVEN.

Dogs pant up to 300 times a minute.

A group of rhinos is called a crash.

A company in India made a

58-FOOT-WIDE (17.7-m)

pair of underpants—
that's wider than three large SUVs.

Ants have lived on Earth for some 140 million years.

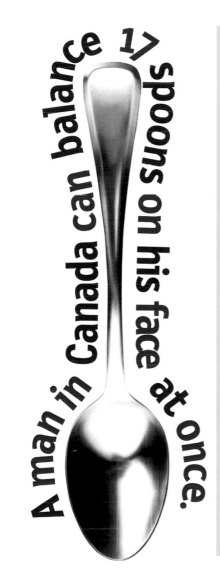

A man in Canada can balance 17 spoons on his face at once.

A rooster is also called a **chanticleer.**

CHEWING GUM WHILE TAKING A TEST MAY IMPROVE YOUR TEST SCORE, ACCORDING TO ONE STUDY.

A canary **can sing two different songs** at the same time.

RAW TERMITES TASTE LIKE PINEAPPLE.

The scientific name for a gorilla is *Gorilla gorilla.*

The
star-nosed **mole**
can find
and eat a
snack
in **230**
milliseconds—
faster than
any other animal.

ZUUL CRURIVASTATOR, a newly discovered species of dinosaur, **was named for an evil monster in the 1984 MOVIE** *GHOSTBUSTERS*.

A TRAIN in Sweden was named **TRAINY McTRAINFACE.**

At Dubai Miracle Garden in the United Arab Emirates, a **full-size model of a jet** is covered in more than 500,000 flowers and living plants.

A FAMILY OF GEESE got a POLICE ESCORT WHILE WADDLING DOWN A HIGHWAY in Colorado, U.S.A.

"SMART BILLBOARDS" IN JAPAN **CAN TARGET ADS AT SPECIFIC DRIVERS.**

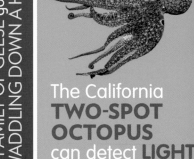

The California **TWO-SPOT OCTOPUS** can detect **LIGHT** with its **SKIN.**

ART STUDENTS IN TAIWAN **MADE POPSICLES FROM POLLUTED WATER** TO RAISE AWARENESS ABOUT POLLUTION.

The **MAORI PEOPLE** of **NEW ZEALAND** refer to the **WETA INSECT** as **"THE GOD OF UGLY THINGS."**

CUCAMELON = a grape-size fruit that looks like a watermelon

THE PEOPLE IN **BRITAIN** DRINK **60 BILLION** CUPS OF TEA EVERY YEAR.

During the 1930s, LIBRARIANS **DELIVERED BOOKS ON HORSEBACK** to people in rural KENTUCKY, U.S.A.

That's Weird!

In the **19th century,** HOCKEY PLAYERS USED **SQUARE PUCKS.**

EATING PUMPKIN SEEDS helps **OSTRICHES** get rid of **PARASITES.**

Honeybees have hair on their eyeballs.

YOUR SENSE OF SMELL IS WEAKER IN THE MORNING AND STRONGER IN THE EVENING.

Sneakers dipped in 18-karat gold once sold for $4,053.

VOLCANIC ERUPTIONS CAN CARRY DIAMONDS TO THE EARTH'S SURFACE.

A man once made **956** pancakes in one hour.

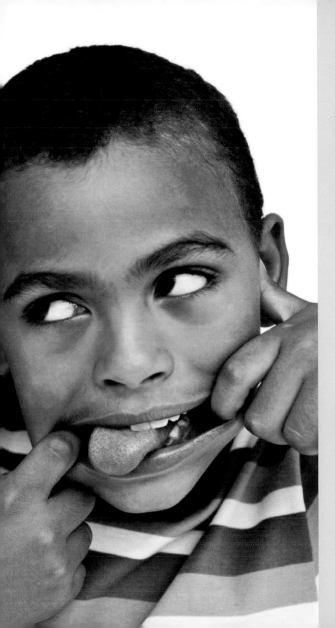

YOUR
TONGUE
PRINT
IS AS
UNIQUE
AS YOUR
FINGER-
PRINTS.

131

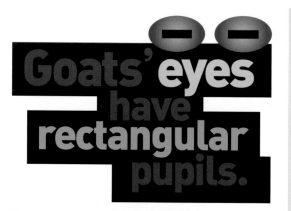

Goats' eyes have rectangular pupils.

A British man ate 36 cockroaches in 1 minute.

SOME SPIDERS CATCH AND EAT FISH.

One of the world's most expensive coffees comes from animal droppings.

Birds
don't
sweat.

Wombat

shaped.

waste is cube-

Paul the octopus **correctly predicted that Spain would win the** 2010 World Cup.

A SALMON'S SENSE OF SMELL IS THOUSANDS OF TIMES BETTER THAN A DOG'S.

Baby **alligators bark** when they are ready to hatch **out of their eggs.**

135

A group of seagulls is

called a squabble.

Some parrots dance when they hear music.

138

6009 is the next year that will look the same right side up and upside down; the last one was **1961.**

YOUR **TEETH** ARE HARDER THAN YOUR BONES.

An inventor created a cell phone that recharges on Coca-Cola.

A housefly can turn somersaults in the air.

An inventor created edible dinner plates.

A tightrope walker is

A restaurant in Taiwan serves **food** in bowls shaped like **toilets.**

A 57-year-old ball of twine weighs **19,000** pounds— (8,618 kg) that's heavier than three hippopotamuses!

called a **funambulist.**

The tallest wave to reach land was taller than the Empire State Building.

HERRING COMMUNICATE BY PASSING GAS.

An **ortanique** is a cross between a **tangerine** and an **orange**.

300 MILLION YEARS AGO, SIX-FOOT-LONG (1.8-m)

A snail can **crawl** along the edge of a **razor** without **cutting** itself.

MOSQUITOES PREFER TO BITE PEOPLE WITH SMELLY FEET.

FAN FACT! SUBMITTED BY LINDSEY Y., 11

MILLIPEDES ROAMED THE EARTH.

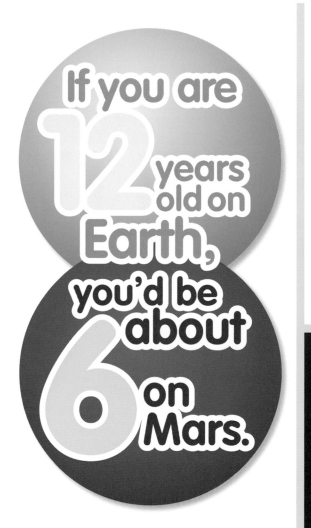

If you are **12** years old on Earth, you'd be about **6** on Mars.

Some tree snakes **glide** up to **78 feet** (24 m) through the air.

THAT'S THE LENGTH OF TWO LARGE SCHOOL BUSES.

Mexico City has sunk 26 feet in the last **100 years.**

You can buy an inflatable TV screen.

The temperature on the moon can be hotter than boiling water.

147

148

THE
DEAD
SEA
IS SEVEN
TIMES
SALTIER
THAN THE
OCEAN.

Tiny bugs live in your eyebrows.

FAN FACT! SUBMITTED BY MARVIN P., 8

Saturn would float in water.

Some pigs are afraid of mud.

Male
seahorses
give birth.

APPLES FLOAT BUT PEARS SINK.

More than 70% of the Earth's surface is water.

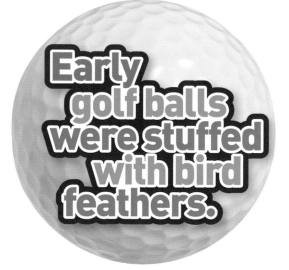

Early golf balls were stuffed with bird feathers.

LARGE FOREST FIRES CAN CREATE TORNADOES MADE OF FLAMES.

▲ **FAN FACT!** SUBMITTED BY JESSICA M., 9

A fifteen-year-old **cat** has probably spent **ten years** of its life **sleeping.**

A giant fungus in Oregon, U.S.A., spreads out over an area the size of **20,000** basketball courts.

Some monkeys in Thailand teach their young to floss.

MALE PLATYPUSES CAN STING YOU WITH THEIR FEET.

THERE ARE SOLID GOLD, PIZZA-SIZE CANADIAN COINS WORTH ONE MILLION CANADIAN DOLLARS.

LAWS IN ENGLAND WERE WRITTEN IN FRENCH FOR MORE THAN 400 YEARS.

Bat hair HAS BEEN USED AS money.

FAN FACT! SUBMITTED BY TAYMAR W., 14

A Russian man drove a **tractor** more than **13,000 miles in 19 days**— (20,900 km) that's longer than the distance from London, England, to Los Angeles, California, U.S.A.

SOME VILLAGES IN POLAND HAVE MORE STORKS THAN PEOPLE.

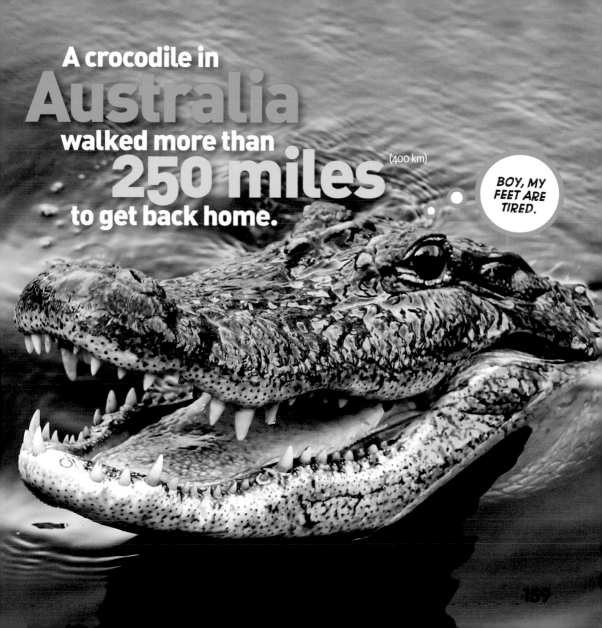

ANTARCTICA

IS A DESERT.

A Finnish man wrote a novel

made up of

1,000 text messages.

You can shine your shoes with a banana peel.

AUSTRALIA'S **GREAT BARRIER REEF** CAN BE SEEN FROM SPACE.

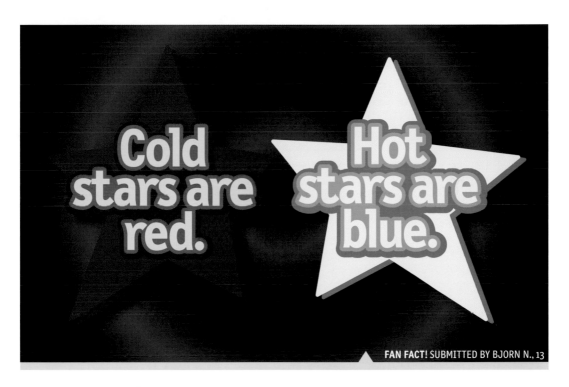

Cold stars are red.

Hot stars are blue.

FAN FACT! SUBMITTED BY BJORN N., 13

Some lizards can **walk on water.**

An artist in New York City opened a **CONVENIENCE STORE** made entirely of **HANDMADE FELT PRODUCTS.**

The **BRIDE** of a **WORLD WAR II SOLDIER** had her **WEDDING DRESS** made from a **PARACHUTE** that SAVED HER HUSBAND'S LIFE.

A group of **STINGRAYS** is called a **FEVER.**

For **$1,400** you can buy an **18-karat-gold** bracelet shaped like the **LEAFY VEGETABLE KALE.**

THE SUN LOSES 4.6 MILLION TONS (4.2 million t) **OF ITS MASS EVERY SECOND.**

When they're feeding, **SEAHORSES** make the **SOUND OF LIPS SMACKING.**

164

OTTAWA, CANADA, hosts winter **DRAGON BOAT RACES** on the ice.

An OFFICIAL U.S. POSTAGE STAMP features a **TOTAL SOLAR ECLIPSE** that **CHANGES TO A MOON** when you put your finger on it.

Your **SHOELACE KNOTS WITHSTAND MORE FORCE WHEN YOU RUN** than your body does when you're **RIDING A ROLLER COASTER!**

SCIENTISTS DESIGNED A ROBOT that **EXTRACTS VENOM** from **SCORPIONS.**

That's Weird!

The **MOROCCAN FLIC-FLAC SPIDER** travels by doing **CARTWHEELS.**

The **AFRICAN PUFF ADDER SNAKE STICKS OUT ITS WORMLIKE TONGUE** to **LURE FROGS AND TOADS.**

You can buy
bat droppings
for about
$10
a pound.

Chewing gum while peeling onions may keep you from crying.

The tallest
known living
man
is
8 feet, (246 cm)
1 inch tall—

a foot and a half (45.7 cm)
taller
than an average pro
basketball player.

IT TAKES 8 MINUTES AND 19 SECONDS FOR LIGHT TO TRAVEL FROM THE SUN TO EARTH.

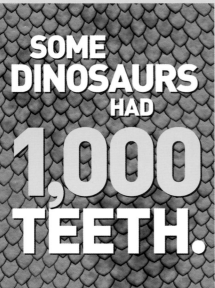

SOME DINOSAURS HAD 1,000 TEETH.

ADULTS HAVE AS MANY AS 1,500 DREAMS A YEAR.

A farmer in Lebanon grew a 25-pound (11-kg) **potato.** That's the weight of two bowling balls!

Bees can be green, blue, or red.

FAN FACT!
SUBMITTED BY CARLY L., 11

The world's largest swimming pool, in Chile, stretches for half a mile.

(0.8 km)

A
flamingo
can eat only
when its head
**is upside
down.**

A HOUND DOG NAMED TIGGER HAD EARS THAT WERE EACH

14 INCHES LONG—

(35.6 cm)

THAT'S LONGER THAN TWO OF THESE BOOKS SIDE BY SIDE.

Almonds belong to the rose family.

A company once sold insurance that covered people in case of injury from a falling coconut.

FAN FACT! SUBMITTED BY MCKENZIE B., 12

SOME MAKEUP HAS FISH SCALES IN IT.

BABIES' CRIES CAN SOUND DIFFERENT IN DIFFERENT LANGUAGES.

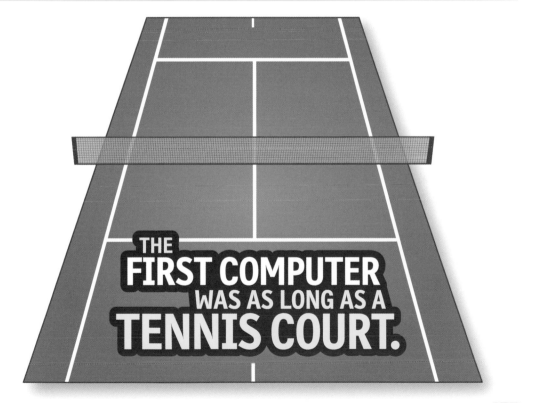

THE FIRST COMPUTER WAS AS LONG AS A TENNIS COURT.

The sound of **waves crashing** comes mostly from **air bubbles.**

A Scottish dish called haggis is cooked inside a sheep's stomach.

Rainbow-colored grasshoppers live in the rain forests of Peru.

A TRAFFIC JAM IN CHINA LASTED

FOR MORE THAN A WEEK.

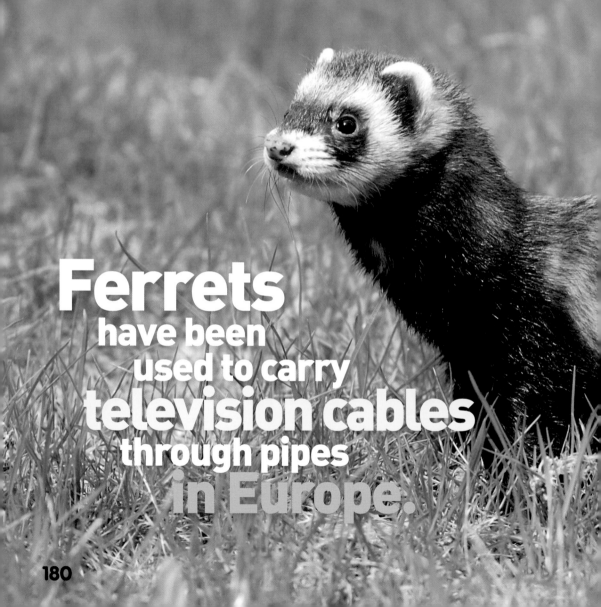

Ferrets
have been
used to carry
television cables
through pipes
in Europe.

THE SHORTEST PROFESSIONAL **BASEBALL PLAYER** WAS **3** FEET, **7** INCHES (109 cm) **TALL,** THE HEIGHT OF AN **AVERAGE** 5-YEAR-OLD.

FAN FACT! SUBMITTED BY JACKSON G., 11

If you never **cut your hair,** it would likely stop growing at about **two feet long.** (61 cm)

SOME **BIRDS** CAN USE THEIR **BILLS** TO MEASURE THE TEMPERATURE OF THEIR **NESTS.**

A MAN DRESSED AS SANTA CLAUS WENT SKYDIVING OVER THE NORTH POLE.

Half the world's oxygen is made in the ocean.

YOU ARE MORE LIKELY TO BE IN A BAD MOOD ON THURSDAYS, ACCORDING TO ONE STUDY.

Brain cells live longer than all of the other cells in your body.

A FIVE-SEAT BICYCLE IS CALLED A **QUINDEM.**

THERE ARE MORE SPECIES OF BEETLES ON EARTH THAN OF ANY OTHER CREATURE.

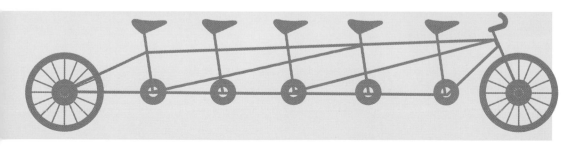

A BUILDING IN POLAND LOOKS LIKE IT'S MELTING.

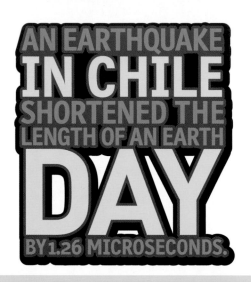

AN EARTHQUAKE **IN CHILE** SHORTENED THE LENGTH OF AN EARTH **DAY** BY 1.26 MICROSECONDS.

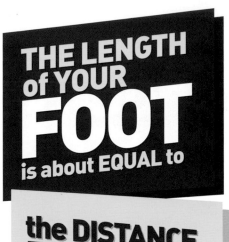

THE LENGTH of YOUR **FOOT** is about EQUAL to

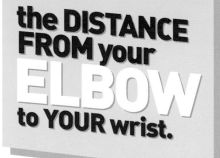

the DISTANCE FROM your **ELBOW** to YOUR wrist.

There is no time at the center of a black hole.

FAN FACT! SUBMITTED BY MILES J., 10

L A C H A N O P H O B I A

is the fear of vegetables.

YOU CAN COMPETE IN AN underwater mountain bike race IN WALES, UNITED KINGDOM.

A sailfish can leap through the air at 68 miles an hour— (109 km/h)
that's about the speed a car drives on the highway.

THERE ARE ABOUT 70 LAKES HIDDEN UNDER THE ANTARCTIC ICE.

Leeches can live in your nose.

Some baby birds use claws on their wings to climb trees.

There are mushrooms that **glow** in the **dark.**

PUG + BEAGLE

PUGGLE

Rotten
eggs
float in
water.

BARBIE'S PETS
HAVE INCLUDED A
LION, PARROT, AND GIRAFFE.

FAN FACT! SUBMITTED BY AUDREY LU M., 14

You can write about 45,000 words with an average pencil.

Penguins swim up to 3,100 miles in a year. (5,000 km)

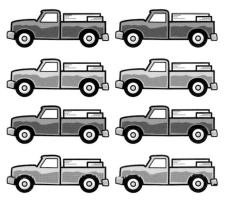

THE INFORMATION STORED ON AN iPOD NANO WOULD FILL UP EIGHT PICKUP TRUCKLOADS OF PAPER.

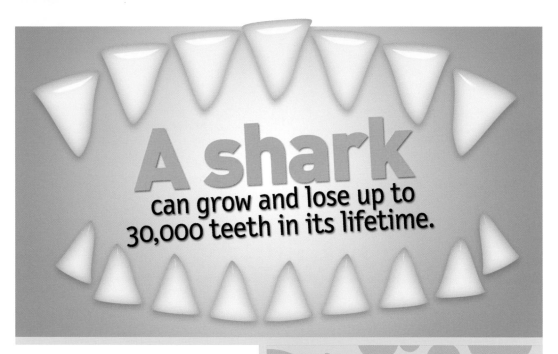

A shark

can grow and lose up to 30,000 teeth in its lifetime.

HARMLESS MICROSCOPIC SHRIMP MAY LIVE IN YOUR DRINKING WATER.

Some artists use chewing gum to make paintings.

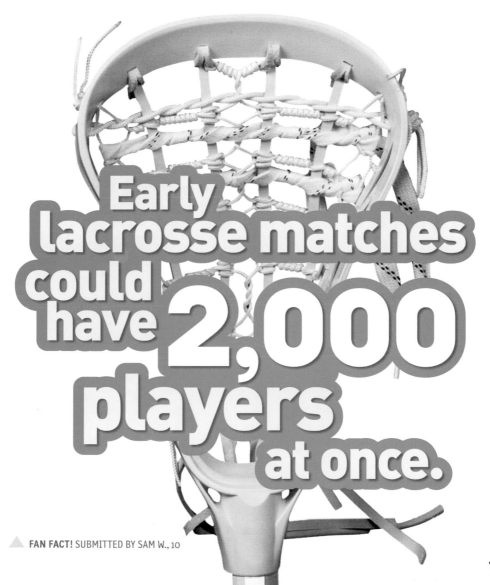

Early lacrosse matches could have **2,000** players at once.

▲ FAN FACT! SUBMITTED BY SAM W., 10

197

A British candy company created a giant box of chocolates filled with

220

.052

individual candies

There is a museum devoted to **ramen noodles** in Japan.

SOME TURTLES BREATHE THROUGH THEIR REAR ENDS.

FAN FACT!
SUBMITTED BY
ANNA M., 8

Woodpeckers once pecked holes in the space shuttle.

BALD EAGLES CAN SWIM.

Some dinosaur eggs weighed more than 10 pounds.

(4.5 kg)

FAN FACT!
SUBMITTED BY
THOMAS D., 10

A BIRD CALLED THE ARCTIC TERN FLIES MORE THAN A MILLION MILES (1.6 million km) **IN ITS LIFETIME—**

THAT'S THE SAME DISTANCE AS MAKING **THREE ROUND-TRIP** FLIGHTS TO THE MOON.

FAN FACT! SUBMITTED BY ZAID A., 11

Circus workers call the toilet a doniker.

It takes **713 GALLONS OF WATER** (2,700 L) to make one cotton T-shirt.

203

ZOOKEEPERS
ARE BITTEN

MORE OFTEN
BY ZEBRAS
THAN BY
TIGERS.

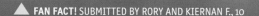 **FAN FACT!** SUBMITTED BY RORY AND KIERNAN F., 10

205

A Chinese man can **blow up** **balloons** using his **ears.**

It's not possible to TICKLE yourself.

GUESS WHAT?

A house flew two miles into the air!
HOW?

Crocodiles eat rocks!
WHY?

Pluto Platter is the original name of this popular, well-known toy!
WHAT?

WANNA FIND OUT?

The FUN doesn't have to end here! Find these far-out facts and more in *Weird But True! 4.*

NATIONAL GEOGRAPHIC KIDS

Weird but true!

That's Weird!

4

350 OUTRAGEOUS FACTS

FACTFINDER

Boldface indicates illustrations.

FACTFINDER

FACTFINDER